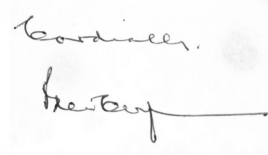

Books by Bennett Cerf

OUT ON A LIMERICK

THE LAUGH'S ON ME

THE LIFE OF THE PARTY

GOOD FOR A LAUGH

LAUGHTER, INCORPORATED

SHAKE WELL BEFORE USING

ANYTHING FOR A LAUGH

LAUGHING STOCK

TRY AND STOP ME

POCKETBOOK OF WAR HUMOR

Books Edited by Bennett Cerf

READING FOR PLEASURE

AN ENCYCLOPEDIA OF MODERN AMERICAN
HUMOR

BEDSIDE BOOK OF FAMOUS BRITISH STORIES

BEDSIDE BOOK OF FAMOUS AMERICAN STORIES

Children's Books by Bennett Cerf

BEGINNER BOOK OF LAUGHS

BEGINNER BOOK OF RIDDLES

MORE RIDDLES FOR BEGINNERS

RIDDLE-
DE-DEE

RIDDLE-

458 - Count Them - 458

Riddles, Old and New, for

Children from 12 to 112

Illustrated by

TOMI UNGERER

DE-DEE

Collected by

BENNETT CERF

Random House   New York

FIRST PRINTING

© *Copyright, 1962, by Bennett Cerf*

All rights reserved under International and Pan-American Copyright Conventions. Published in New York by Random House, Inc., and simultaneously in Toronto, Canada, by Random House of Canada. Limited.

Library of Congress Catalog Card Number: 62–16285

Manufactured in the United States of America by

Design by Tere LoPrete

Life's perhaps the only riddle that
We shrink from giving up.
—W. S. GILBERT

Contents

Introduction

I had always been aware of the fact that children liked riddles. Just how much they liked them, however, I didn't realize until two years ago, when I compiled a book of riddles designed for boys and girls of five or six who were beginning to learn to read by themselves.

We just couldn't keep that darn book in print: It and a follow-up collection, named, reasonably enough, *More Riddles*, have to date sold almost a half a million copies, and no end is in sight. Furthermore, the parents of the wee ones for whom the books were designed very obviously were getting just as much pleasure out of the riddles as their offspring were.

So why not, I reasoned, get to work on a much more comprehensive collection of riddles, intended for children from sixty-five to one hundred and twelve as well as five to twelve—riddles that might be a bit beyond the comprehension of the latter at first glance, but that could be explained to them when their elders had stopped groaning.

I discovered that although no reasonably adult collection like this had been attempted for

11

thirty years and more, the riddle has played a definite role in the passing parade for centuries. The *Cambridge Bibliography of English Literature* lists collections dating all the way back to 1511 —probably containing some of the very riddles included herewith!

Folklore, in fact, is liberally sprinkled with riddles, many of which are quite unfathomable today. Most famous of them, of course, was posed by the Sphinx, a winged lion, according to Greek mythology, with the head of a woman. The Sphinx lived on a high rock outside of Thebes and demanded of anyone rash enough to come within earshot, "What walks on four legs in the morning, two at noon, and three in the evening?" The punishment she meted out to those who couldn't answer was on the drastic side: she killed them.

Finally, however, Oedipus confounded her by answering correctly, "Man. He crawls on all fours as a babe, walks upright in the prime of life, and uses a staff in old age." The Sphinx was so mortified that she varied the usual procedure— and killed *herself!* Oedipus thereupon became King of Thebes.

The next famous figure who resorted to riddles, we are told, was Strongman Samson. In the Old Testament—Book of Judges, 14:14—Samson suddenly stopped thirty companions in their tracks with "Out of the eater came forth meat, and out of the strong came forth sweetness." In three days, the Bible proclaims, the thirty companions could not expound the riddle—which is not too surprising, since the wily Samson had neglected to supply the pertinent facts. It developed that he had just come from killing a young lion within whose carcass he had discovered a swarm of bees and honey: he had eaten some of the lion and some of the honey.

Skipping two thousand years and more, we find that Abraham Lincoln frequently resorted to riddling when a political argument threatened to get out of hand. "How many legs will a sheep have if you call the tail a leg?" he suddenly demanded of one adversary who maintained that Negroes in the South really were living under "protection" and not in "slavery." "Five," answered that surprised gentleman. "Four," contradicted President Lincoln, "for calling a tail a leg does not make it one."

Aficionados are cautioned about guessing the correct answers to other people's riddles too quickly. Children especially like to confound their elders. You will increase their pleasure immeasurably if you fail to come up with the right answer to a riddle, no matter how often they repeat it to you.

They tell of a famous scholar who found himself sharing a seat in a slow coach with a farmer and proposed an exchange of riddles to help pass the time away. "When I miss a riddle," suggested the scholar, "I'll pay you a dollar, but since obviously I've had more opportunity than you to acquire knowledge, when you miss a riddle you need pay me only fifty cents."

The farmer nodded agreement. "I have my first riddle ready for you right now," he said. "What is it that weighs six hundred pounds on the ground and only fifteen when it flies?" "I don't know," confessed the scholar, "so here's my dollar." "I don't know either," admitted the farmer—and handed back fifty cents.

Veteran riddle fanciers will find plenty of chestnuts in the pages that follow—but there are a great many new ones for you, too. School kids these days are an inventive lot—and they seem to favor puns as much as I do. Furthermore, as I have so often discovered with puns, the more outrageous the riddle, the more vociferous its reception is likely to be.

Riddle away!

Bennett Cerf

RANDOM HOUSE
NEW YORK
JUNE 1962

RIDDLE-DE-DEE

The Birds and the
Beasts Are Here

Q. What did the duck say when it laid a square egg?

A. "Ouch!"

Q. Why do hummingbirds hum?

A. Because they don't know the words.

Q. What's the difference between a bird with one wing and a bird with two wings?

A. A difference of a pinion.

Q. Why do birds fly South?

A. Because it's too far to walk.

Q. What did the duckling say when he saw his first colored Easter egg?

A. "Ooh, look at the orange marmalade."

Q. What do they call a duck who garners nothing but A's on his report card?

A. A wise quacker.

Q. Why does a baby duck walk softly?

A. Because he can't walk, hardly.

Q. Why was Farmer Wimpfheimer's rooster named Robinson?

A. Because he Crusoe.

Q. How can you keep a rooster from crowing on Sunday morning?

A. By killing him on Saturday night.

Q. What happens when you cross a bulldog with a Plymouth Rock hen?

A. The hen lays pooched eggs.

Q. Why is a hen immortal?

A. Because her son never sets.

Q. Why would a compliment from a chicken be an insult?

A. Because it would be in foul language.

Q. How might a man and a goose in a disabled airplane get down without a parachute?

A. He could pluck the goose.

Q. If you planted an angry crow, what would come up?

A. Crow-cusses.

Q. If ten birds were sitting on a telegraph wire and you shot one, how many would be left?

A. None. The others would all fly away.

Q. What should a man know before trying to teach a dog?

A. More than the dog.

Q. Which has more legs—a dachshund or no dachshund?

A. No dachshund. No dachshund has eight legs; a dachshund has only four.

Q. How can you know when it's raining cats and dogs?

A. Step into a poodle.

Q. Why is a dog's tail like the heart of a tree?

A. It's farthest from the bark.

Q. What are two good names for a dog kennel?

A. 1. A barking lot. 2. Chock Full o' Mutts.

Q. Why is a dog biting his own tail like an efficient housewife?

A. He is making both ends meet.

Q. What do people in Hollywood call young gray cats?

A. Kittens.

Q. What is a kitten after it's three days old?

A. Four days old.

Q. How do you make a Maltese cross?

A. Pull its tail.

Q. What happens when you give a cat lemons?

A. You get a mighty sour puss.

Q. How do you make a slow horse fast?

A. Stop feeding him.

Q. What kind of a horse can take several thousand people for a ride at the same time?

A. A race horse.

Q. What has four legs, eats oats, has a tail, and sees equally well from both ends?

A. A blind horse.

Q. What animal has eyes that cannot see, legs that cannot move, but can jump as high as the Empire State Building?

A. A wooden horse. (The Empire State Building cannot jump.)

Q. How do you get a horse out of a bathtub?

A. Pull out the plug.

Q. Why is a horse halfway through a gate like a cent?

A. Because his head's on one side; his tail's on the other.

Q. What is even more remarkable than a horse that can count?

A. A spelling bee.

Q. What do they call a bee that buzzes around filling stations?

A. An Esso bee.

Q. Why did the fly fly?

A. Because the spider spied-er.

Q. What's the happiest day in the life of a young mosquito?
A. The day it passes its screen test.

Q. Why did the moth eat the rug?
A. To see the floor show.

Q. Why did the exterminator hide his head every time a moth cried?
A. Because he couldn't bear to see a moth bawl.

Q. When is a mother flea saddest?
A. When her children go to the dogs.

Q. When does a caterpillar improve its morals?
A. When it turns over a new leaf.

Q. What does a worm do in a cornfield?
A. Goes in one ear and out the other.

Q. What do you call a rabbit who has never
been out of the house?

A. An ingrown hare.

Q. Why is a rabbit's nose usually shiny?

A. Because he has the powder puff at the wrong
end.

Q. How can you find a lost rabbit?

A. Make a noise like a carrot.

Q. When Baby Rabbit asks Mama Rabbit,
"How did I come into the world?" what does
Mama Rabbit answer?

A. "A magician pulled you out of a hat."

Q. Ask me if I'm a rabbit.
A. Okay. Are you a rabbit?
Q. Yes, I'm a rabbit. Now ask me if I'm an alligator.
A. I'm game. Are you an alligator?
Q. No, you loon. I told you I'm a rabbit.

Q. When is an auto not an auto?
A. When it turns turtle.

Q. When is a frog unable to talk?
A. When he's got a man in his throat.

Q. What is the difference between a cat and a frog?
A. A cat has only nine lives; a frog croaks every minute.

Q. How can you keep fish from smelling?

A. Cut off their noses.

Q. How can you tell a gentleman sardine from a lady sardine?

A. Observe which can it comes out of.

Q. What two animals go everywhere you go?

A. Your calves.

Q. When was beef the highest?

A. When the cow jumped over the moon.

Q. What is the first thing a farmer must remember?

A. Never try to milk a bull.

Q. Why does a baby pig eat so much?

A. To make a hog of himself.

Q. Why are hogs like trees?

A. Because they root for a living.

Q. Why is a pig's tail like getting up at 4:40 A.M.?

A. It's twirly.

Q. What might you say to a pig that was weeping?

A. Porc-u-pine.

Q. What did one pig say when he held down another pig?

A. "I won't let you up till you say oinkel."

Q. What have you got when you collect 100 female pigs and 100 male deer?

A. Two hundred sows and bucks.

Q. What's the best time for a farmer to look over his pigs?

A. When he has a sty in his eye.

Q. What is the best butter in America?

A. A goat.

Q. When does a ram burst out sobbing?

A. When he hears somebody on the radio singing "There'll Never Be Another Ewe."

Q. If a postmaster went to a circus and a lion ate him, what time would it be?

A. Ate P.M.

Q. What's black and white and red all over?

A. A blushing zebra.

Q. Why are elephants gray?

A. So you can tell them from blueberries.

Q. What is the difference between an elephant and a flea?

A. An elephant can have fleas, but a flea can't have elephants.

Q. How do you get down from an elephant?

A. You don't get down from an elephant. You get down from a duck.

Q. How can you tell a male rhinoceros from a female rhinoceros?

A. Ask it a question. If *he* answers, it's a male; if *she* answers, it's a female.

Q. What is dark underneath, white on top, and very warm in hot weather?

A. A wolf in sheep's clothing.

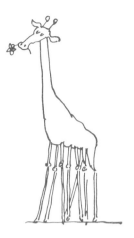

Q. When do giraffes have eight legs?

A. When there are two of them.

Q. What do giraffes have that no other animal has?

A. Little giraffes.

Q. What is worse than a giraffe with a sore neck?

A. A centipede with athlete's foot.

Q. What's the difference between a zoo and a delicatessen?

A. In a zoo you can see a man-eating lion and a man-eating tiger, but you have to go to a delicatessen to see a man eating herring.

31

Q. What did the near-sighted porcupine say when it backed into a cactus?

A. "Pardon me, honey."

Q. What three keys have legs but won't open doors?

A. Monkeys, donkeys, and turkeys.

Q. Why do some monkeys sell potato chips?

A. Because they're chip monks.

Q. If you wake up in the middle of two lions, three elephants, four leopards, and five tigers, what should you do?

A. Stop the merry-go-round and get off.

Whee, the People!

Q. What's the best thing to take when you're run down?

A. The license number of the car that hit you.

Q. How can you fall over forty feet without getting hurt?

A. Move from the front to the rear of a crowded bus.

Q. How can you always find a liar out?

A. Go to his office when you know he isn't in.

Q. A man fell out of a tenth-story window but was barely scratched. Why?

A. He was wearing a light fall suit.

Q. How can you avoid falling hair?

A. Jump out of the way.

Q. How can you get into a locked house, with all the windows tightly barred, without a key?

A. Keep running around the house until you're all in.

Q. What's the real reason men and women go to nudist camps?

A. To air their differences.

Q. What happened when the boarding house blew up?

A. Roomers were flying.

Q. Why is your nose in the middle of your face?

A. Because it's the scenter.

Q. What sense pleases you most in a dreary bore?

A. Absence.

Q. Four men fell into the water, but only three of them got their hair wet. Why?

A. One of them was bald.

Q. What happens when the human body is submerged in water?

A. The telephone rings.

Q. Who are the men who most often make their mark?

A. The ones who can't write.

Q. If a man is born in Switzerland, grows up in Ghana, comes to America, and dies in Ashtabula, what is he?

A. Dead.

Q. What did American players prove when they won the English bridge championship four years running?

A. London Bridge Is Falling Down.

Q. How many girls would reach from New York to Philadelphia?

A. About ninety-five, a miss being as good as a mile.

Q. What are the three most common causes of forest fires?

A. Men, women, and children.

Q. Why was Society called the "Four" Hundred?

A. Because it was two, two.

Q. Why did the FBI keep Slugger O'Keefe and Squinty Carmichael's fingerprint records at opposite ends of their files?

A. Because they were whorls apart.

Q. When does the captain of a yacht get a traffic ticket for careless piloting?

A. When he sails past a red lighthouse.

Q. What was the best student at the Agricultural College voted by his classmates?

A. "The kid most likely to sack seed."

Q. What is a perfectionist?

A. A man who takes infinite pains—and usually gives them to everybody around him.

How-to-Do-It
Riddles

Q. How can you make a locomotive sit down?
A. Remove its tender behind.

Q. What's the easiest way to double your money?
A. Fold it.

Q. How can you divide sixteen apples among seventeen hungry people?
A. Make applesauce.

Q.   What is the best material for kites?

A.   Flypaper.

Q.   A barrel weighed twenty pounds. A man put something in it and then it weighed only ten pounds. What did the man put in it?

A.   A hole.

Q.   How can you make pants last?

A.   Make the coats and vests first.

Q.   If you awaken in the middle of the night in a strange bed, and are thirsty, what should you do?

A.   Look under the mattress and find the spring.

Q.   How can you make one pound of coffee go as far as a hundred pounds of tea?

A.   Buy the above quantities in New York and ship them to Seattle.

Q. What time is it when the clock strikes thirteen?

A. Time to get the clock fixed.

Q. What's a good thing to part with?

A. A comb.

Q. How can you make a dollar fast?

A. Nail it to the table.

Q. How can you make a thirsty Scotsman's tongue turn black?

A. Drop a bottle of brandy on a freshly tarred road.

Q. What Roman numeral can you make climb a wall?

A. IV.

Q.   Why do they have mirrors on chewing-gum
     machines?

A.   So you can see how you look when the gum
     doesn't come out.

Alike and Unalike

Q. Why is a swaggering dictator like a harp
    struck by lightning?
A. Because both are blasted lyres.

Q. Why is a dirty man like flannel?
A. Because he shrinks from washing.

Q. Why is a stick of candy like a race horse?
A. Because the faster you lick it, the quicker it
    goes.

Q. Why is a straw hat like kissing over the phone?

A. Because neither is felt.

Q. Why is a burning cigarette like a race-track tout?

A. Because they both have hot tips.

Q. What gives a cold, cures a cold, and pays the doctor's bill?

A. A draught.

Q. Why is a watch like a river?

A. Because it doesn't run long without winding.

Q. Why is a pair of skates like an apple?

A. Because both are responsible for the fall of man.

Q. Why is a man sailing up the Tigris like a scoundrel stuffing his father into a sack?

A. Because they both are aiming to Bag-dad.

Q. Why is mince pie eaten on an ocean liner like a difficult conundrum?

A. Because one is frequently obliged to give it up.

Q. What did a very long-winded taxi driver have in common with a visitor to Waikiki Beach?

A. They both got Cerf bored riding.

Q. What's the difference between a diplomat and a hot dog?

A. A diplomat wears full dress; a hot dog just pants.

Q. What's the difference between a gardener and a billiard marker?

A. One watches his peas; the other his cues.

Q. What's the difference between a chess champion and a pickpocket?

A. One watches pawns; the other pawns watches.

Q. What's the difference between a furious circus owner and a Roman barber?

A. A circus owner is a raving showman; the other is a shaving Roman.

Q. What's the difference between a dog and a sailor who harpoons a whale?

A. The dog wags his tail; the sailor tags his whale.

Q. What's the difference between a Dutch half-wit and a piece of stovepipe?

A. One's a silly Hollander; the other's a hollow cylinder.

Q. What's the difference between Little Goldilocks and a genealogist?

A. A genealogist is interested in forebears.

Q. What's the difference between yachtsmen and shad?

A. Yachtsmen sail, but shad roe.

Q. What's the difference between an Irishman frozen to death and a Scotsman at the North Pole?

A. One is kilt with the cold; the other cold with the kilt.

Q. What's the difference between a man struck with amazement and a leopard's tail?

A. One is rooted to the spot; the other is spotted to the root.

Q. What's the difference between a bee and a donkey?

A. One gets all the honey; the other all the whacks.

48

Q.   What's the difference between a fly and a mosquito?

A.   You can't sew a zipper on a mosquito.

Q.   What was the difference between Noah's Ark and Joan of Arc?

A.   One was made of wood; the other was Maid of Orléans.

Q.   What's the difference between a teen-ager and a pillow?

A.   The teen-ager is hard up; the pillow is soft down.

Q. What's the difference between Elizabeth Taylor and a mouse?

A. One charms hes; the other harms cheese.

Q. What's the difference between a Swiss and a jailer?

A. One sells watches; the other watches cells.

Q. What's the difference between a fisherman and a lazy schoolboy?

A. One baits his hooks; the other hates his books.

Q. What's the difference between a man going up the stairs, and one looking up?

A. One steps up the stairs; the other stares up the steps.

Q. What's the difference between the Milky
    Way and a roomful of great-grandfathers?
A. One is a lot of pale stars; the other a lot of
    stale pas.

Q. What's the difference between a poet and
    an astronomer?
A. A poet tries to get his head in the heavens;
    an astronomer tries to get the heavens in his
    head.

Q. What's the difference between a pessimist
    and an optimist?
A. A pessimist is a female who's afraid she
    won't be able to squeeze her car into a very
    small parking space. An optimist is a male
    who thinks she won't try.

Riddles for
Romantics

Q. Why do young lovers usually stick to each other like glue?

A. Because the feeling is mucilage.

Q. What two beaux can no girl get rid of?

A. Her elbows.

Q. When do ships grow affectionate?

A. When they hug the shore.

Q. When is a hat not a hat?
A. When it becomes a pretty girl.

Q. How can a girl hold on to her boy friend's love?
A. By not returning it.

Q. Why is an octogenarian better able than a young leading man to keep a chorus girl warm?
A. Because there's no fuel like an old fuel.

Q. Where can you find girls who won't neck in cars?
A. The woods are full of them.

Q. Why is a short man trying to kiss a tall girl like an Irishman climbing Mt. Vesuvius?

A. Because, sure, he's trying to get to the mouth of the crater!

Q. Why do old maids wear mittens?

A. To keep off the chaps.

Q. What succession of miracles occurred when Irving Stone and Grant Wood watched Marilyn Monroe pass by?

A. Stone turned to Wood. Then Wood turned to Stone. Then both of them turned to rubber. Then Miss Monroe turned into a movie studio.

Q. What happened when a ticket seller and the girl who ran the information booth went up to the top floor of Grand Central to be pronounced man and wife by a justice of the peace?

A. They married above their station.

Q. Why is a girl who's been a bride for exactly five minutes like a melon?

A. Canteloupe.

It's All in the Family

Q. How can you always keep three jumps ahead of your wife?

A. Play checkers with her.

Q. Why do we call our language the mother tongue?

A. Because Father never gets a chance to use it.

Q. What's the surest way for a husband to incense his wife?

A. Pull the wool over her eyes with the wrong yarn.

Q. What is it that no man wants, but once he has it, never can bear to lose?

A. A bald head.

Q. What is the best way to prevent water coming into your house?

A. Don't pay your water tax.

Q. When does a wife become a magician?

A. When she turns an old rake into a lawn mower.

Q. What is the easiest breakfast to take in bed?

A. A couple of rolls.

Q. When is it socially correct to serve milk in a saucer?

A. When you're feeding the cat.

Q. What is a counter irritant?

A. A lady shopping.

Q. On what day of the year do women talk least?

A. On the shortest day of the year.

Q. How old would a baby girl, born in 1920, be today?

A. Twenty-nine.

Q. What do women do with the years they take off their true ages?

A. They add them to the ages of their best friends.

Q. What's a good line for announcing the birth of a baby daughter?

A. "We have skirted the issue."

Q. Which is bigger: Mr. Bigger or Mr. Bigger's
baby?
A. The baby is a little Bigger.

Q. What frequently happens when an electric
shaver marries a doorbell?
A. They have a little humdinger.

Q. How did Mrs. Smith have triplets one
Monday, and twins a week later?
A. One of the triplets got lost.

Q. Why do some babies' hair turn snow-white
at the age of three months?
A. They have near-sighted mothers—who keep
powdering the wrong end.

Q. What's the best way to drive a baby buggy?

A. Tickle his feet.

Q. How can you stop a small child from spilling food at the table?

A. Feed him on the floor.

Q. What was the father doing when he tore a copy of *The Wisdom of India* from his two-year-old son's clutches?

A. Taking Gandhi from a baby.

Q. Why do older boys often offer to help with their baby brothers' diapers?

A. It's a sure way to make a little change.

Q. What happens to little girls who swallow bullets?

A. Their hair comes out in bangs.

Q. Why are promises like noisy brats at the movies?
A. Because the sooner they are carried out, the better.

Q. If you throw a juvenile delinquent in the water, what does he become?
A. Wet.

Q. In a young boy, what is cleanliness next to?
A. Impossible.

Q. When should a boy kick about something he gets for his birthday?
A. When he gets a football.

Q. What did the mother say when she learned that her son had consumed thirty-seven batter cakes at one sitting?

A. "How waffle!"

Q. If a man should give one son fifteen cents and another ten cents, what time would it be?

A. A quarter to two.

Q. When a little boy puts his socks on wrong side out, what does his mother do?

A. Turns the hose on him.

Q. Why did the boy stand behind the donkey?

A. He thought he'd get a kick out of it.

Q. Are clubs any good for children?

A. Only when kindness fails.

Q. Why should girls never learn a foreign language?

A. Because one tongue is enough for any woman.

Q. Why did a mother knit her G.I. son three socks?

A. Because he wrote that he had grown another foot.

Q. Why is a son at college like an electrician?

A. Because they both wire constantly for money.

Q. What happens to a girl who doesn't know cold cream from putty?

A. All her windows fall out.

Q. How do you make anti-freeze?

A. Take away her pajamas.

Eat, Drink, and Be Merry

Q. What book has the most stirring chapters?

A. A cook book.

Q. Who won the world's all-time eating championship?

A. The man who bolted the door, swallowed a story whole, and then threw up a window.

Q. Who has the most friends for lunch?

A. A cannibal.

Q. What is brought frequently to the table, then cut, but never eaten?

A. A pack of cards.

Q. When was the little strawberry upset?

A. When his ma and pa were in a jam.

Q. What's worse than finding a worm in an apple?

A. Finding half a worm.

Q. Which side of an apple pie is the left side?

A. The side that isn't eaten.

Q. If you were walking alongside a jackass, what fruit would you represent?

A. A pear.

Q. If you see three ripe tomatoes lined up on a shelf, which one of them is a cowboy?

A. None of them. They're all redskins.

Q. What makes a tomato red?

A. It blushes to see the salad dressing.

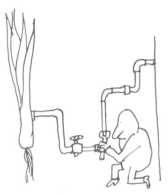

Q. What vegetable always needs a plumber?

A. A leek.

Q. What goes up white and comes down yellow and white?

A. An egg.

Q. How can you buy eggs and be certain there are no chickens inside them?

A. Buy duck eggs.

Q. If eggs were twenty-six cents a dozen, how many could you buy for a cent and a quarter?

A. Twelve.

Q. What's the smallest room in the world?

A. A mushroom.

Q. What stands on one leg with its heart in its head?

A. Lettuce.

Q. What is there more of after you've eaten it than before you touched it?

A. An artichoke.

Q. What food is dear at any price?

A. Venison.

Q. What is the difference between a tuna fish and a piano?

A. You can't tune a fish.

Q. What is larger than a nutmeg?

A. A nutmeg grater.

Q. What nut reminds you of a sneeze?

A. A cashew nut.

Q. When should a baker quit making doughnuts?

A. When he gets sick of the hole business.

Q. What did the bridegroom do when his wife made him a marble cake?

A. He took it for granite.

Q. What did the little boy say to the lollipop?

A. "I can lick you any day."

Q. What has only one horn, is white, and gives milk?

A. A milk truck.

Q. What's the best way to keep milk from turning sour?

A. Keep it inside the cow.

Q. What do you do if you get vinegar in your ear?

A. Suffer from pickled hearing.

Q. What is a coquette?

A. A small Coca-Cola.

Q. What's the purpose of a cocktail called "The Ark"?

A. It's for people who can't say Noah.

The Old Familiar
Places

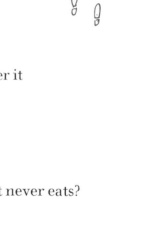

Q. How can you tell when a train is gone?
A. It leaves its tracks behind.

Q. What is a drop of sea water after it
    graduates from college?
A. Fit to be tide.

Q. What has a mouth and fork but never eats?
A. A river.

Q. Name a product raised in countries where
    there's lots of rain.
A. Umbrellas.

Q. What has four legs and one foot?

A. A bed.

Q. What was the largest island in the world before Australia was discovered?

A. Australia.

Q. Where were the first doughnuts made?

A. In Greece.

Q. What makes the Tower of Pisa lean?

A. It doesn't eat enough.

Q. What did the plane traveler over the Riviera say?

A. That's Nice.

Q. What parts of Berlin are in France?
A. The letters *r* and *n*.

Q. What's the richest country in the world?
A. Ireland—because its capital is always Dublin.

Q. When is a Scotsman like a donkey?
A. When he walks by the banks and braes.

Q. How many big men have been born in New York?
A. None. Only babies.

Q. Why does the Statue of Liberty stand in New York?
A. Because it cannot sit down.

Q. What's the coldest place in the Yankee Stadium?

A. Z-row.

Q. Why is it bad to look at Niagara Falls too long?

A. You may get a cataract in your eye.

Q. What's the best thing to do if you find Chicago, Ill.?

A. Summon a Baltimore, M.D.

Q. What city's name signifies the greatest exhibition of strength ever given in the United States?

A. Wheeling, West Virginia.

Q. What has four eyes and runs more than two thousand miles?

A. The Mississippi.

Q. Name the twelve most appropriately named towns in America.

A. Shapeless, Mass.; Ooola, La.; Goodness, Me.; Income, Tex.; Deathly, Ill.; Hittor, Miss.; Praise, Ala.; Coco, Colo.; Proan, Conn.; Farmerina, Del.; Inert, Mass.; and Hezmakinizeatme, Pa.

Q. What four states would a well-dressed boy be wise to visit?

A. North D-COAT-a, PANTSylvania, VEST Virginia, and COLLAR-ado. (He might also tarry at these cities on his way home: TIE-conderoga, C-HAT-tanooga, Delaware Water CAP, and SHOE-x City.)

Q. What do they call an ice-cream vendor in Arizona?

A. A good Yuma man.

Q. What did Tennessee?

A. Precisely what Arkansas.

Q. What do they call the cabs lined up at airports and railroad terminals?

A. The yellow rows of taxis.

Q. What do they call a man in Texas who is six feet tall?

A. A midget.

Occupational Hazards

Q. Why must a doctor keep his temper?

A. He can't afford to lose his patients.

Q. Why is a dead doctor like a dead duck?

A. Because they both have stopped quacking.

Q. Why did the doctor put the debutante in a
    private room?

A. Because she was too cute for wards.

Q. Why is a surgeon who doesn't drink like a shipyard?

A. Because he is a dry doc.

Q. Why did the little boy tiptoe past the medicine chest?

A. He was afraid he'd awaken the sleeping pills.

Q. What pain do we make light of?

A. Windowpane.

Q. How can you prevent getting a sharp pain in the eye every time you drink a cup of coffee?

A. Take the spoon out of your cup.

Q. Is writing on an empty stomach harmful?

A. No, but paper is better.

Q. How can you live to be one hundred years old?

A. Drink a glass of milk every morning for twelve hundred months.

Q. A Tasmanian, a Bulgarian, and a Hottentot all applied for the same job at the U.N. one day. The director said he'd engage the man who could climb highest up the side of the building. All three fell off. Who got the job?
A. The undertaker.

Q. What time did the Chinese scholar go to the dentist?
A. Tooth hurty.

Q. Why do dentists get fat?
A. Practically everything they touch is filling.

Q. What's the best way to catch a squirrel?
A. Climb a tree and act like a nut.

79

Q. Who was the unluckiest tree surgeon?
A. The one who kept falling out of his patients.

Q. Why do most janitors marry young?
A. They sweep girls off their feet.

Q. What asks no questions but requires many answers?
A. A doorbell.

Q. Why doesn't a maid eat her apron?
A. It goes against her stomach.

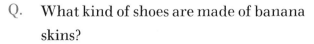

Q. What kind of shoes are made of banana skins?
A. Slippers.

Q. What coat is made without sleeves and put on wet?
A. A coat of paint.

Q. What do you call the suspension of activity in a real estate subdivision brought about by an acute shortage of funds?
A. A case of arrested development.

Q. Why do absconding cashiers usually head for Canada?
A. Because that's the only place they have Toronto.

Q. What comes out when you palm off a lead nickel at the Automat?
A. The manager.

Q. What's behind the stars?
A. Policemen.

Q. Why is a postman like a bigamist?
A. Because they both ring twice.

Q. Why is a traffic cop the strongest man in the world?

A. Because he can hold up a ten-ton truck with one hand.

Q. Why does a traffic signal turn red?

A. You would, too, if you had to change in front of all those people.

Q. If a man smashed a clock, could he be convicted of killing time?

A. Not if the clock struck first.

Q. Why don't candle trimmers work from Monday through Friday?

A. Because they just work on wick ends.

Q. What are a chorus girl's favorite winter sports?
A. Rich ones.

Q. What has eighteen legs and catches flies?
A. A baseball team.

Q. What man shaves more than twenty times a day?
A. The barber.

Q. What often starts a fight on a train?
A. When the conductor punches the tickets.

Q. If an athlete gets athlete's foot, what does an astronaut get?
A. Missile toe.

Q. Why do drama critics usually praise the first play of a new season?

A. They don't want to stone the first cast.

Q. Why does a political candidate need three hats?

A. He needs one to wear, one to throw in the ring, and one to talk through.

Q. What's the one thing in the world that can never be beaten?

A. A broken drum.

Q. What's the hardest thing to deal with?

A. An old deck of cards.

Q. What are the hardest kind of beans to raise on a farm?

A. Jelly beans.

Q. What turns without moving?

A. Milk.

Q. What always works with something in its eye?

A. A needle.

Q. What works when it plays, and plays when it works?

A. A fountain.

Q. What contains more feet in winter than in summer?

A. A skating rink.

Q. What runs but never walks?

A. A river.

Q. When is a sailor not a sailor?
A. When he's aboard.

Q. What thing is lengthened by being cut at both ends?
A. A ditch.

Q. How can you locate a good lady inventor?
A. You can't. They've all been hiding since the day they invented ladies.

Q. How did an impecunious professor defend his habit of borrowing money from all other members of the faculty?
A. He explained that he was working his way through colleagues.

Q. Why did the wine-tester's wife buy an automobile?
A. So she could drive her husband to drink.

History: Hot Off the Riddle

Q. What did the swan say when he flew down from Olympus and landed in Greece?

A. "Take me to your Leda."

Q. What was the principal contribution to civilization made by the Phoenicians?

A. Phoenician blinds.

Q. When Brutus asked Caesar, "How many hot dogs did you eat at the Forum today?" what did Caesar answer?

A. "Et tu, Brute."

Q. Name two ancient sports.

A. Antony and Cleopatra.

Q. Why did the suits of armor worn by King Arthur and his knights cost at least five cents an ounce?

A. They were first-class mail.

Q. How did Henry VIII differ from other suitors?

A. He married his wives first and axed them afterwards.

Q. What character in Shakespeare killed the most ducks and chickens?

A. Hamlet's uncle, because "he did murder most foul."

Q. What bus crossed the ocean?

A. Columbus.

Q. Why did Robin Hood rob only the rich?

A. Because the poor had no money.

Q. For what was Louis XIV chiefly responsible?

A. Louis XV.

Q. Why wouldn't Emperor Maximilian climb the Alps?

A. Because he was an anti-climb-Max.

Q. Who took the first taxicab ride in American history?

A. George Washington, when he took a hack at the cherry tree.

Q. Why is it useless to send a letter to Washington today?

A. Because he died in 1799.

Q. Who introduced the pendulum in America?

A. Pendulum Franklin.

Q. Where was the Declaration of Independence signed?

A. At the bottom.

Q. Why isn't ten cents worth what it once was?

A. Because dimes have changed.

Q. Of what trade are all the presidents of the U.S.A.?

A. Cabinet makers.

Q. Why did the old Confederate soldier bring his rifle to the ball park?

A. He heard the Yankees were playing.

Q. What's the first thing a statesman must learn today?

A. How to watch his appease and accuse.

Q. What subway train should Truman and Eisenhower use?

A. An ex-Pres.

Q. Why did Eisenhower move to a farm in Pennsylvania?

A. Because, like Lincoln, he wanted a Gettysburg address.

Q. What made Francis Scott Key famous?

A. He knew all the verses of "The Star-Spangled Banner."

Q. Why is President Kennedy like "The Star-Spangled Banner"?

A. Because he is the national him.

Sunday Morning Riddles...

Q. Who didn't hang up his clothes when he went to bed?

A. Adam.

Q. Who was the first man mentioned in the Bible?

A. Chap. One.

Q. Who was the first girl mentioned in the Bible?

A. Gene-sis.

Q. At what time was Adam created?

A. A little before Eve.

Q. What did Adam first plant in the Garden of Eden?

A. His foot.

Q. What was the cause of Adam's first real argument with Eve?

A. He caught her putting his best Sunday suit into the salad.

Q. When was the first time walking sticks popped up in the Bible?

A. When Eve presented Adam with a little Cain.

Q. How many apples were eaten in the Garden of Eden?

A. Eve ate, and Adam, too, and the devil won. That makes eleven in all.

Q. How were Adam and Eve prevented from gambling?

A. Their pair o' dice was taken away from them.

Q. Why didn't the ancients use slates and pencils?

A. Because the Lord told them to multiply on the face of the earth.

Q. What did Noah say when the animals started climbing into the Ark?

A. "Now I herd everything!"

Q. What animals failed to come to Noah's Ark in pairs?

A. Worms. They came in apples.

Q. Where was Noah when the lights went out?

A. In d'ark.

Q. Why didn't they play cards on the Ark?
A. Because Noah was sitting on the deck.

Q. Where did Noah keep his bees?
A. In the ark hives.

Q. What did the stuttering cat say when he looked out the window of Noah's Ark?
A. "Is that Ararat?"

Q. When was paper money first mentioned in the Bible?
A. When the dove brought green back to Noah.

Q. When did Abraham sleep five in a bed?
A. When he slept with his forefathers.

Q. When were cigarettes first mentioned in the Bible?

A. When Rebecca saw Isaac and lighted off the camel. (Genesis 24.)

Q. Who was the best businesswoman in the Bible?

A. Pharaoh's daughter. She drew a prophet from a rush on the bank.

Q. Where did Moses' baby clothes come from?

A. Jordan Marsh.

Q. When was the first tennis game in the Bible?

A. When Moses served in Pharaoh's court.

Q. If you were to throw a white stone into the Red Sea, what would it become?

A. Wet.

Q. Who was the greatest actor in the Bible?

A. Samson. He brought down the house.

Q. Where was Solomon's Temple?

A. On the side of his head.

Q. How did Jonah feel when the whale swallowed him?

A. Down in the mouth.

Q. Why is snow different from Sunday?

A. Because it can fall on any day of the week.

Q. What is a minister doing when he rehearses his sermon?

A. Practicing what he preaches.

Q. Why are sinners like potatoes and corn?
A. Because they have eyes, yet see not, and ears, yet hear not.

Q. If a woman were to change her sex, what religion would she then represent?
A. She would be a he'then.

Q. Why are there so few men with whiskers in heaven?
A. Because most men get in by a close shave.

Q. Why is a good riddle like a church bell?
A. Because it is frequently tolled.

... And Pun-Day Afternoon Riddles

Q. Why is a strip teaser like a prophet?

A. Because she has not much on-'er in her own country.

Q. What seats does a theatre manager like best?

A. Receipts.

Q. Why did the beautiful girl keep pulling at her clothing?

A. Because she was a chafing dish.

Q. What did the woman say when the maid spilled an iced beverage down her front?

A. "Careful, Audrey—this isn't a tea vee."

Q. When Shakespeare asked Anne Hathaway if the moths had gotten at his last year's evening cape, what did she say?

A. "No holes, Bard."

Q. What is a panther?

A. A man who makes panth.

Q. How could you refer to a tailor whose name you had forgotten?

A. As Mr. Sew-and-sew.

Q. What did the big toe say to the little toe?

A. "Don't look now, but there's a heel following us."

Q. What did the Irishman tell the chiropodist?

A. "Me fate is in your hands."

Q. Why is it a good idea to take a hammer to bed with you?

A. So you can hit the hay.

Q. What do you call a man who lends his tools to a neighbor?

A. A saw loser.

Q. What did the gardener say when his flowers wouldn't bloom?

A. "Upsadaisy!"

Q. How can you shoot 120 hares with one bullet?

A. Fire at a wig.

Q. How much land is like a decaying tooth?

A. An acre.

Q. What usually happens when two peanuts go out for a walk?

A. One is a salted.

Q. Why did the tramp demand ten dollars for one cup of coffee?

A. He was putting all his begs in one ask-it.

Q. What kind of servants are best for hotels?

A. The inn-experienced.

Q. Why is Fido like a positive creed, Pa?

A. Because he's a dog, Ma.

Q. What is worse than raining cats and dogs?

A. Hailing taxicabs.

Q. When is silence all wet?

A. When it reigns.

Q. What color is a ghost?

A. Boo!

Q. What color is a marriage?

A. Wed.

Q. When are the police detailed to City Hall lawn?

A. When the grass begins to shoot.

Q. What happens when a reformed gangster studies spiritualism?

A. He goes from bad to medium.

Q. When is a letter damp?

A. When it has postage dew.

Q. What did the ballpoint pen say to the paper?
A. "I dot my eyes on you."

Q. When is a nose not a nose?
A. When it's a little reddish.

Q. Why did the pine tree pine?
A. Because it saw the weeping willow weep.

Q. How many insects does it take to make a landlord?
A. Ten-ants.

Q. When does a candle feel hot?
A. When it has glowing pains.

Q. Why wasn't the painter burned when he shoved his arm into the paint remover?
A. Because the hand was quicker than the lye.

Q. When are pipes like humbugs?

A. When they're meerschaums.

Q. What did one tonsil say to the other tonsil?

A. "Better get dressed. The doctor's taking us out tonight."

Q. Why is a speech delivered on the flight deck of a carrier like a lady's costume jewelry?

A. Because it is a deck-oration.

Q. What did the skeptic say to the inventor of the steam engine?

A. "So, Watt."

Q. What distinguished author does this represent? Mrs. Jones and her daughter operate a chicken farm. Mrs. Jones sends said daughter out to check on the number of eggs the hens have laid one morning. Daughter reports in a speech of four syllables.

A. Some are set, Marm.

Q. What famous novel does this represent? Groucho and Harpo Marx dash into a room where two mothers are boasting about their offspring, sling the bewildered ladies over their shoulders, and kidnap them.

A. The Brothers Carry Mas Off.

Q. When Mr. Kissinger changed his name to O'Brien, and then to Schnickelheimer, what did all his friends go round saying?

A. "I wonder who's Kissinger now."

Q. What four island names are complete questions?

A. Hawaii? Jamaica? Samoa? S'TATen Island?

Q. When is a Pakistani unhappy?

A. When he's Sikh, Sikh, Sikh!

Q. If a train, with a Norwegian at the throttle, approaches at full speed, and a train, with a drunk at the throttle, comes from the opposite direction on the same track, and still there is no collision, what does this prove?

A. That Norse is Norse, and souse is souse, and never the twains shall meet.

Stormy Weather

Q. Why does an Indian wear feathers?

A. To keep his wigwam.

Q. Why are hurricanes named after girls?

A. Because they're not himicanes.

Q. Why did the weather forecaster get bounced from his job?

A. The climate didn't agree with him.

Q. Which is faster: heat or cold?

A. Heat. You can catch cold.

Q. Why is a flea like a long winter?

A. It makes a backward spring.

Q. When are eyes not eyes?

A. When the cold air makes them water.

Q. How can you keep a dog from going mad in August?

A. Shoot him in July.

Q. What bow can never be tied?

A. A rainbow.

Q. What sort of day would be the best for running for a cup?

A. A muggy one.

Q. If you spot a Cherokee seeking a ride on the highway, what season is it?

A. Indian thumber.

Q. Why isn't the moon rich?

A. Because it spends its quarters getting full.

Q. What animal drops from the clouds?

A. The rain, dear.

Q. Why does lightning shock people?

A. Because it doesn't know how to conduct itself.

Q. Why are most fathers like rainbows?

A. Because they appear after the storm is over.

Q. When does the rain become too familiar to a lady?

A. When it begins to patter behind.

Q. What's the first thing that turns green in the spring?

A. Christmas jewelry.

Q. Why is autumn the best time for a lazy gent to read this riddle book?

A. Because autumn will turn the leaves for him.

Take My Words for It

What should you do if you catch a dog eating your desk dictionary?

A. Take the words right out of his mouth.

Q. What question can *never* be answered "Yes"?

A. "Are you asleep?"

Q. What question invariably *demands* "yes" for an answer?

A. "What does Y-E-S spell?"

Q. Who said, "I'm going to give you a big squeeze when I meet you on the bridge tonight"?

A. A toothbrush—talking to the toothpaste.

Q. What did the big flower say to the little flower?

A. "Hiya, bud."

Q. What does an acorn say when it grows up?

A. "Geometry."

Q. What did the big chimney say to the little chimney?

A. "You're too young to smoke."

Q. What do they call folks who never return borrowed riddle books?

A. Bookkeepers.

Q. What did the rake say to the hoe?
A. "Hi, hoe."

Q. Where does Monday come before Sunday?
A. In the dictionary.

Q. What is broken by merely naming it?
A. Silence.

Q. What word of three syllables contains twenty-six letters?
A. Alphabet.

Q. Do you know any word composed entirely of vowels?
A. Aye.

Q. Why is D a bad boy?
A. He makes ma mad.

Q. What is the end of everything?
A. The letter G.

Q. What two letters spell jealousy?
A. NV.

Q. What's the noisiest vowel?
A. O. All the others are in audible.

Q. What one letter in the alphabet will spell the
word potato?
A. The letter O. Put them down one at a time
until you have put eight o's.

Q. What comes after "O"?
A. Yeah.

Q. What word becomes shorter when a syllable is added to it?

A. The word short.

Q. What's the longest word in the dictionary?

A. Smile. (There's a mile between the first and the last letter.)

Q. When is a river like the letter "T"?

A. When it is crossed.

Q. Is there one word that contains all the vowels?

A. Unquestionably.

Q. What word is always pronounced wrong?

A. Wrong.

Q. How can you prove that seven is half of twelve?

A. Draw a line across XII and leave VII.

Q. If joy is the opposite of sorrow, what is the opposite of woe?

A. Giddyap.

Q. How much does the sub-weigh?

A. Two tons: down-ton and up-ton.

Q. Define the following in words that rhyme:

1.	A false timepiece.	A.	Mock clock.
2.	His Majesty's possessions.	A.	King's things.
3.	A note and a dog.	A.	Letter, setter.
4.	A New York depository for choice spirits.	A.	Knickerbocker liquor locker.

Do you know Humphrey?   Humphrey who?
Humphrey ever blowing bubbles.

Do you know Sam?   Sam who?   Sam
Enchanted Evening.

Do you know Sarah?   Sarah who?   Sarah
doctor in the house?

Do you know Ira?   Ira who?   Ira member
Mama.

Do you know Hugh?   Hugh who?   Hugh who
to you, too.

Do you know Max?   Max who?   Max little
difference.

Do you know Karloff?   Karloff who?   Karloff
my dreams, I love you.

Do you know Tarzan?   Tarzan who?   Tarzan
stripes forever.

Do you know Chester?   Chester who?   Chester
minute and I'll see.

Do you know Kerch?   Kerch who?   Gesundheit.

Do you know Celeste?   Celeste who?   Celeste
time I'll ask you.

Do you know Della?   Della who?   Della
Katessen.

Do you know Wendy? Wendy Who?
Wendy Moon Comes Over de Mountain.

Do you know Thelma? Thelma Who?
Thelma, Pretty Maiden, Are There Any More
at Home Like You?

Can you use these words in sentences?

ARCHAIC
We can't have archaic and eat it too.

LOQUACIOUS
She bumped into me and I told her to loquacious
going.

MACHIAVELLI
My pa'll machiavelli good pair of pants for ten
dollars.

PARADOX
On our farm we have four chickens, six geese,
and a paradox.

CONSCIENCE STRICKEN
Don't conscience stricken before they're hatched.

BEWITCHES
I'll bewitches in a minute.

MERETRICIOUS
I wish you a meretricious and a happy new year!

And—signing off—

Q. Do you know what part of a whale is like
this book?

A. Certainly! It's

FINIS